Rainbows of Stone

Volume 43

Sun Tracks

An American Indian Literary Series

Rainbows of Stone

Ralph Salisbury

THE UNIVERSITY OF ARIZONA PRESS   TUCSON

The University of Arizona Press
© 2000 Ralph Salisbury
First Printing

☉ This book is printed on acid-free, archival-quality paper.
Manufactured in the United States of America

05 04 03 02 01 00   6 5 4 3 2 1

Library of Congress Cataloging-in-Publication Data
Salisbury, Ralph J.
Rainbows of stone / Ralph Salisbury.
p.   cm. — (Sun tracks ; . 43)
ISBN 0-8165-2036-4 (pbk. : alk. paper)
1. Indians of North America—Poetry.   I. Title.   II. Series.
PS501 .S85   vol. 43
[PS3569.A4597]
811'.54—dc21
99-050462

British Library Cataloguing-in-Publication Data
A catalogue record for this book is available from the British
Library.

Publication of this book was made possible in part by
a grant from the National Endowment for the Arts.

This book is, as all of my writing has been,

dedicated to my children and grandchildren;

to my other family members; to all my people,

Indian and Caucasian; and to the human tribe of

this world. I wish to express gratitude to the young

writers who have been my students. From their

heroic endeavors I have learned and am still

learning. I would like to make a special dedication

to my wife, Ingrid Wendt, who has been my lover

and comrade for thirty years. Her poems and

person illuminate and warm my days.

Contents

IV *Death Songs*

Because of poverty and because of growing up in the remote hills to which white men with guns had driven our Indian people, my father had only two years of school. As a traveling minstrel, a gifted singer, self-taught to play five-string banjo, my father performed in many of the states of America. The G.I. Bill of Rights, enacted into law during my first year of military service in World War Two, partially paid for my education through a Master of Fine Arts Degree. As a writer, I have continued in the oral tradition, reading from my work and talking and telling stories in North America, Europe, and India.

Some Native American writers know and write of the reservation life or of urban Indian life. I need to recall the vanishing farming and hunting traditions with which I was raised. They are the landmarks I need if I am to keep to the Medicine Path I feel is mine. Because I have lived the vestiges of Indian ways possible in my time, ways that are less and less possible to live, I often speak through the persona of an Indian, but I am both Caucasian—gray eyes—and Indian— no longer black-haired and no longer misperceived to be Italian or Jewish but still possessed of Indian cheekbones, under my wrinkled hide, and still employing my own "spade-shape Indian incisors" to bite meat and corn. I am not, as my family name suggests, an English American, certainly not an heir to the Salisbury earldom and not in line to be the first American Bishop of Salisbury. I am not, as the U.S. government decrees, part Indian—one fourth—and not part white— three fourths. In a story called "War," Luigi Pirandello's character says of sons killed, "[A] father does not give half of his love to one son, half to another. He gives all of his love to each son." I would give all of my love to my Indian people and all of my love to my white people. I am not part Indian, part white, but wholly both.

At 73, a grateful survivor of machines' and their controllers' intentions or imperfections, my own mistakes, some animal attacks, some human attacks, a few bullets, explosions, and illnesses, I know that much of what I have lived will pass from the human story with my passing, but in the hope that I may leave the earth something more than one hundred fifty pounds of fertilizer, I have based my life's work on my own, my family's, and others' experiences.

Rainbows of Stone is not meant to be a verse autobiography, but it begins with poems of childhood, moves to increasing awareness of our world, and ends with my natural awareness that my long life must inevitably soon end. Throughout the book, I have sought to evoke that which is good and to be enjoyed in life, and that which is evil and to be resisted, attacked, and destroyed.

In my daily prayers I thank the Creator for my small place in all the immensity, power, glory, and beauty of Creation. I pray that I may be worthy of my Medicine Path and live well enough and long enough to fulfill my destiny. In this spirit, I humbly offer yet another book to anyone who may choose or chance to read it, and I pray that it may be of some value. *Ha yi yu,* may it be so, may it be so, may it be so, may it be so.

I

Leaving My People

I learn by going how I have to go.
  from "The Waking," by Theodore Roethke

A Declaration, Not of Independence

for my mother and father

Apparently I'm Mom's immaculately-conceived
Irish-American son, because,
Social-Security time come,
my Cherokee dad could not prove he'd been born.

He could pay taxes, though,
financing troops, who'd conquered our land,
and could go to jail,
the time he had to shoot or die,
by a Caucasian attacker's knife.

Eluding recreational killers' calendar's
enforcers, while hunting my family's food,
I thought what the hunted think,
so that I ate, not only meat
but the days of wild animals fed by the days
of seeds, themselves eating earth's
aeons of lives, fed by the sun,
rising and falling, as quail,
hurtling through sky,

fell, from gun-powder, come—
as the First Americans came—
from Asia.

Explosions in cannon,
I have an English name,
a German-Chilean-American wife
and could live a white life,

but, with this hand,
with which I write, I dug,
my sixteenth summer, a winter's supply of yams out
of hard, battlefield clay,
dug for my father's mother, who—
abandoned by her husband—raised,
alone, a mixed-blood family
and raised—her tongue spading air—
ancestors, a winter's supply or more.

Being Indian

Who we were seemed simple when gun
dropped meat onto plates, but,
a pistol, in the hand
which had patted my head,
our wood-box as full
as I could get it, dropped
a drunk dead, blade falling from white fist—

next story prison, where,
a straight-razor swung, "Guts
slithered like snakes,"
as Dad's might have done,
if a lawyer had not convinced the governor
to pardon an Indian.

The path to Granny's apples and tales
Turkey Creek's bramble-tangled bank;
the road snow, mud or dust, from my parents' farm,
to redskin-plundering Carnegie's free—
now tax-supported—library—war,
for national survival through colonial tyranny,
was my Medicine Way into the 20th Century,
being what I was not ever simple again.

Family Task, 4th Year

for my sister Ruth, who shared in this, as in so much

Like small ancestors, red
as dawn in storm, white
as first frost on window, I
have cradled the small
in small arms bent, as the small,
themselves, had to bend,
between rigid bigger, to grow,
to help grown trees to strive,
against others taller still, into light,

the small to kindle blaze and throw,
from small toes' ends,
my monster shadow—black
as the time after prayer, when sun
is gone, maybe not ever to return—
dancing, in twigs' crackling rhythm,
over the living-room's familiar
cold floor's slivers, further than one could see,
into scary dark.

First Kill, 4th Year

for my friend Jack, USAF, b. 1925, d. 1945

I have asked, small voice
an echo of hunter ancestors', or—
his son his future—Dad
has fitted my finger, thin
as the sick chicken's claw,
around trigger curved like beak of hawk.

Eighteen, a friend in burning bomber, a gun
his only salvation
from pain—thousands of feet
too far for a bullet to reach—four
again—and seventy now—I aim muzzle, bright
as Tooth Fairy dime,
between wings, and, when
Dad speaks a wisdom all of us have,
buried within, no stronger than my Creator,
I give the last possible gift
given me to give.

As Straight As

Following Sunday's decapitation,
evisceration, frying and prayer before
milk-teeth tore flesh, our war-cry, "War-
bonnets," wing-pluckings rubber-banded around
our scalps, we'd burn
each other or classmates, staked
to the flagpole—but,

above strips flayed, red, from pale,

white-star-emblazoned warplanes aimed
pretend-fire-arrows and shamed—

in soon to be real, black
newspaper-rows,
as straight as history's
blue-jacket-troops'—

the worst stories we'd ever heard.

A Stick-Horse-Indian's History

Forked-twig tomahawk strapped at my side,
astride a red forebear's brown-
barked warhorse, I'd ride where
my brothers were
no longer playing
soldier, far from battlefields
Greatgrampa had plowed, "since,"
he'd said, "the Indians,"
not able to foresee
my Cherokee dad's marrying into the family—

as I—centuries
of cavalry history bearing me—
could not foresee what would be
the end of the road,
the road to the rest of the world,
where my brothers were,
where my brothers were.

Of Pheasant and Blue-Winged Teal

Mother's people, pictured in their stiff black best,
were filed in drawers, but Dad's killed,
buffalo, deer and bear, respectfully, and,
in an oral history
not on school shelves,
defended sacred land
against the White kids' dead,
family hunters and warriors closer to me
than any teacher across a desk,
bone fingers guiding gun dropping rain-
bow glory of pheasant and blue-winged teal
and Nazism's Christian-crossed planes
from sky—ghost tongues lightning from
my own dark tomb.

Lazarus

Mud on his patches, cold
wind raising the blind,
evergreens black
before a last supper-plate's scraped,
he gnaws nails while
my children choose
among candies, and
I find myself
studying a star-
shaped crater, where the tooth
of a bully struck knuckle.

He's gone,
to be a bombardier,
in the loft of a barn,
which would burn and burn
again, in Rotterdam, London, Dresden and Japan; gone
from this bright house,
where family, friends and enemies,
the only human possibilities, come,
bidden or unbidden, but no one,
no one can stay.

Passing Rez School the Day before Thankstaking Day,
Unoriginal Sin and a Redskin Pilgrim's Retrogression

Footpath passing a school,

undiscovered by a nun
black at her blackboard's explanation
of Vanishing Americans' vanishing, I find myself

flagged, by two not quite red rows,
unfurled into grin, two white, and by one
five-pointed, pale star.

My lips let my teeth pledge allegiance,
again, my fingers orbiting their own warmth,
around this pen,
as straight as Old Glory's tall pole, but
admittedly, ingloriously smaller, and,

as the star descends, it draws,
from Christian calendars' precision constellations,
a child—hand cramped
from fisting fact onto dusty black
clutching a wand,
to draw him Everywhere.

Though the teacher scowls
us back to my dead, risen from
The Trail of Tears

as chalk,
this day before Thankstaking Day, a child
will lead, as I finish taking my walk.

Geometry of a Cherokee History

Cylindrical shape of
 the salt-shaker big kids
 told me to take to
 shake on the tail of a bird
 and catch it—

and of
 a tube filled with my blood hung
 on a silver gallows
 beside a hospital bed,
 years later—Dad's

 red cartridges actually caught:

pheasants,
 whose beaks caught bugs;

foxes,
 as red as the shotgun shell that caught them
 raiding our chicken-yard; and

our neighbor,
 who might have been safer robbing, instead,
 the bank, which had robbed him of his farm—
 one side of his head red,
 we heard, from the doctor,
 whose only pay would be
 a memorable story—

its title:
 The Great American Depression—

its ending:
    bomb-smoke, black
    as pepper, shook from
    cylindrical shakers, when monster birds
    caught enemies' kids.

Those Glittering Claws

Beyond concrete streets trussing earth
like a Thankstaking Day turkey,
badger's a black-and-white fact, its den

a secret escape-tunnel-from-castle,

one hill, horizon-small,
the pine-feathered-headdressed head
of a chief, his tribe
ancestors, crossing the Mississippi for
their Southeastern Migration,
forgotten for generations
before The Trail of Tears,

and tongue swims air
risen from river's chill,

mind,
when one thinks about it,
a grave within a cave,

like those in earth,

or sky, stars bats, their glittering claws
prying, relentlessly, gently prying,
trying to open eyes.

Between Bandoliers

"Draw" drawled the sun,
and rain as quick
as any "galoot" drew
from a brown holster I'd called "the ditch"
a real Wild West six-shooter.

Its bullets, though just pellets of rust,
shot hell out of boredom
for fourth grade friends, to whom
any manipulation of time
more emphatic than kilowatt clicks
was a winner. Tick. BANG!

However, the ghost
of that hombre, once downed so easily,
"dry-gulches"—meaning "ambushes"—me,
though irony's said
to be more potent than
a "shooting-iron."

One day, You Posses Formed To Enforce The Possible,
a gun aimed
between bandoliers of words, I fell,
to my knees, ready to be spliced by any God,
and what I've survived, if
nothing
else, is certainty.

Breed Kid's Initiation Rite: 1981

Red vine-maple leaves   bright Christmas lights
    boots glistening under dawn dew   new-
        er than they'd been since the store   last year

his father's car   far
    down mountain   a little stocking-stuffer
        dirt road gray wool

he's twelve   a Cherokee man
    a gun in his hands
        but what

the Deer Prayer gone
    with Grandad
        back into earth

his brothers forced into war
    against strangers
        whose skin-color's similar to his

what
    he's Christianized not
        to question

what
    is it
        he hunts?

Without Thunder

Twelve, I was shocked out of dreams by what
whatever makes thunder had done to the barn
my mother's father, whom I'd only known
as chiseled stone, had built from trees—
last leaves become food
for grass—cows' grazing becoming bones
and teeth, as I drank, every day, without thought.

Fifteen, my father and brothers heard,
thunderbolt's Voice Beyond Words,
and my singed ears tuned-in
silence, more clear than radios' military oratory,
my body the barn, risen from ashes of hay
and animals, to teeter on finger, as in
fevered delirium, at three.

Eighteen and feeling the roller-coaster lift,
a bomber lightened of load, I saw, and I see
what brothers and father saw touch me, and, friends
turned into smoke, I heard,
and I hear, only my own sounds,
failing at becoming understanding.

Leaving the Land

Its rulers taking others' wages for leisure, lives
for war, and oxygen, for more and more cars—
this city's glitters, in smog,

could be glowing coals
of the Yankee-Stadium-
McAllister-Castle-Salisbury-Cathedral-
Roman-Colosseum barn,

which armies had killed whole tribes
and Mother's father had killed
acres of oaks to raise.

Hay-bale-forts we stormed—after school
had massacred our Indian people again,
by ignoring them—turned into smoke
when the Thunder God I venerate as "Red Man" spoke.

Docile though hands had,
year after year,
seemed bigger and bigger mouths
of calves, bovine tons
thinned into buffalo phantoms, while eggs,
I'd have had to search for for days, fried
like flame-plumed Montezuma's less
precious than gold flesh,
between shuddering drumsticks, and colts of colts of colts—
of war-steeds Spaniards bestrode
and bestowed on allies, when taking home slaves and loot
by boat—incinerated into remudas that grazed,
with fossil-fuel's ravening dinosaurs,
ozone's diminishing savannah.

No delicate skeletons to evoke
the Hiroshima horror of brains
sizzling in tiny skulls,
my own brain suffering
no memory of lovingly stroking purring embers
to sleep among cinders—I could say that,
on blistered paw-pads,
my kittens scampered away
childhoods in wilds—
in imagination, grown
to claw fledglings from air,
some years of my life before
one bombardier, in an instant, torched more
than Genghis Khan, Attila the Hun,
Cortéz or Torquemada
on their best days had done.

Unloading

"One thing I will say about you—"

his two huge geldings hauling home, easily,
the mountain of hay my aching arms had raised—
over it, war-eagles, his gold-framed lenses caged,
raging, to one
dreaming of piloting, who the boss was:

his voice, money'd distilled to gin;

his daughter's newest clothes
and the lift of her lovely nose;

his car a meteor blazing past film-star-struck
astronomers groping unbuttoned unknowns in dark
observatories, parked beside the road
to the bare-titty night-club city;

his face as white
as winter-bandaged land
his family had fought
Indians for, and his space
reserved in Christian rows of stone—

bright bombers his, history would show,
though others would labor in them, loading, unloading—

"One thing I will say,
you've been schooled, but
you know your place."

Death of _____ _____, Chief without a Tribe

"Might tipple just a bit," neighbors laughed—
his nose red as a fire-exit bulb—
"but works like a Percheron and a Belgian rolled into one
with two mules thrown in for good measure, although
he's a donkey in size. A Saturday night stallion for sure.
So lock up your liquor and women."

Spring after spring,
earth opened for him
to plant seed deep,

and green he'd freed of weeds

tickling, knee-high by the Fourth of July,

kernels would fill like a pregnant sow's tits
before first frost

turns growth to winter-feed,

planter to hunter, trapper and lover, till spring

turns him to field hand again.

Tribesmen and women and children gone,
with the forests, down,
his nose, a boozy red dawn, rose
over smoky coffee's sobering pow-wow-fire, till night

sprang up,
robed in black flames,
from a last cup,

scaring the shit out of me, for one,
not yet a man, seeing it could come
even for him,

but damned if he didn't offer it a drink,
"One for the road?"—teeth grinning tombstone rows—
and, though obeying its own old Chief's, "Hell no!"
damned if it didn't hesitate,
as if wishing it could say, "o.k."

A Longer

for Robert

"Big hugs from white women," he tells me.

It's dark. We neither one know where we are.

"Thin blouses. My shirt wet with sweat—"

From dragging kids out of wrecked bus.
From fearing fuel might explode.

From knowing they weren't the same color,
those breasts, his chest.

He is not there on that familiar road
to the flick-Coke-and-popcorn town, which held,
also, a school—
is here—returned from war—
on a longer road darker than
graves of our Cherokee ancestors, who, too,
risked everything—as everyone must—
to save what they could, and we
grope through wreckage to save
what we need from them.

Then and Still

for James Boswell, d. 1795,
and for my friend Wiz, d. 1945

The red of scorched blood,
the "Super Flying Fortress
Gunnery Information" booklet I—
"requisitioned" we used to euphemize—stole,
for a souvenir, lies,
an ironic burial-plaque,
on a boxful of family-photo-albums.

My oxygen-mask curls beside it, a worm,
huge-headed like a human foetus, or a gray-green rose,
through whose stem I requisitioned enough breath
to go on uttering the doggerel of those days,

like "Roger" for "yes,
I understand." An 18-year-
old snickerer, I'd live
to learn that "Roger" meant "fuck"
to Boswell's 18th Century's gentry.

Circuitry spaghetti the cook
neglected, electric-machine-gun-tur-
rets jammed—"Situation Normal, All
Fucked Up," we'd say,
abbreviated to "SNAFU."

And "Fucked" was code
for: travel-orders "cut"
in smoke, buddies "requisitioned" by
an "outfit" then,
and still, more secret than
the Atom-Bomb Squadron.

A 20th Century Cherokee's Farewell to Arms

The only good Indian is a dead Indian.
General William Tecumseh Sherman

You sought this—even though lightning had burned

    breath from your lungs
    and careered fence-wire to plunge
    down post as near
    the center of the world you shared
    as it could get—

sought to become the warrior a Cherokee

    might be by being
    a scout for white troops and for
    the God of Christian "civilization," Whose devout's
    guns had converted "savages" into "good Indians."

Your war-path miles

    above the tallest corn—
    you'd later learn
    was as sacred as ancestors it had fed—

from height where lightning had been,

    your scientific killing-skills burned
    Dresden and turned
    into rat-claws flesh where noses of babies born
    in Japan should have been
    receiving oxygen, exhalation giving cherry trees
    impulse to bloom
    and giving the next generation the words
    for mating and praying,

the screams of victims to be
the screams of Cherokees tortured and massacred—and
of all the people who have ever been or will be
lovers or killers.

Green Smoke

"Helicopters?" he asks, long distance. But
I'm Heavy Bombers. It's six in the morning, not nine.
I am Pacific, and he's Atlantic. It's World
War Two again, my sleep destroyed
By rescuers, seeking to rescue one of their own—
A crew-mate with my same name—from oblivion,

And, yes, eighteen, I saved eight men,
Nine if I count myself,
Corralling a bomb banging wild like a colt
Against our own bomb-bay, and now I'm a poet
And try to save everything
I love. But, no;
Grass bursts like green smoke up
From graves of some friends,
And only my best wishes go
To The Rescue Squadron Reunion.

We Are Asked to Understand,

the barman, who's heard it before, and me,
a stranger, ex-soldier, my worst not so bad as this
pilot's, his rocket the same,
to men in a tank, as my friends' bombing plane,
what turned them into meat and cooked it, but
my memory is smoke, vanishing in wind.

Two ears hear,
and two once more,

that a mouth, which had said
what all men say
to sweethearts and wives, spurted blood as hot
as come into crotch,

that, his friend's severed head
between drenched thighs,
our brother has got to keep on flying and shooting
and living the horror, the guilt, the grief
all of us live—or should—
our dead born again
in brains spines join
to loving, suffering flesh,
more precious, more beautiful,
its doom foreknown.

Ahab over Japan

Dinosaur-generations' miles of browse
crushed, by aeons of ocean-fathoms, to fossil-fuel,

a mammal, who cooked but did not eat
his cannibal-kills, sees:

Mt. Fuji as salt-crusted breast,
airliner contrail as umbilical cord,
its red, not blood but dawn,

smoke—not from bomb
but from factory—
an illusion of spume,

Leviathan giving back,
after almost unendurable pressure, a share
of the world's atmosphere, having kept,
like any of our former enemies, or us, enough.

New Years Night, Moss-Hall Tavern, London

for my son Brian

Doctor, I remember best your friend
the height of my thirteen-year-old son
and as drunkenly incoherent as the baby you
certainly were too and those
you tried to treat for burns and those
you merely helped be born
in Hiroshima.
        "Shame.
Shame on your great nation,"
you said and would not hear
how many would have died
in slightly slower fires already turning Tokio
into Honolulu, magnified.

Let your Roman Catholic God
bless all the Samurai,
I say, and let them eternally torture
the crew of the Enola Gay
and me if I should fail
to affirm Shame
on my nation and on
the Samurai said to have nobly
scorned the Potsdam Ultimatum
till after Nagasaki and Shame
on the Russians said to have wanted
at least one atom-bomb and one city of Nippon less
in communism's future—
and, thus, were not lucid couriers—and Shame,
even, on the small laboring man
so drunk he could only try
to utter "Shame" or "Fry all Japs"
whatever it was or might have been.

Yes, Shame, even, on him I remember best of all
because he spit in my face,
his tongue trying hard to tell what he felt
but failing as a courier,
only accidentally expressing something
so just I would not have erased it from my cheek
even if I could have done so
without hurting my unwitting inquisitor's feelings,
nor would I save from humiliation

the face of any human,
not even that of my son,
though he is gentle
and does not want humans in Vietnam burning
themselves or him.

A Cherokee's Second Christening

Ribs wrecked
      and his wife's eye cut
So it wept
      the rest of her life,
"The Iron Man
      With the Automatic Smile"
Was medicine
      white nurses gave a proud Cherokee
To keep on taking at home.

"Survivor of
      the, lost, Indian Wars
      and of a Wrecked Bomber Like
      the One That Bore
A Mother's Name —
      Enola Gay —
      Into History"
One father christens himself,
      this Father's Day, 1980 a.d.

War Over, Blue Heron Ascending

for my brother Bob

Flesh thin as my family's bodies were
once weeks of potatoes, pared so close to rot
they tasted of it, were gone,

thin as dust wind,
first music of Earth,
persuaded from stone,

a blue heron, the only quarry
I'd found, all day, sank
its songless, fish-seeking beak
into the brain of a hunter who'd spared it, out
of brotherly pity or maybe the thought
that it would be like eating his own skinny body.

Today, a survivor, of atoms waked,
from aeons of fasting, to monstrous gluttony,
sees fish become
Blue Heron generations, and bones
of Hiroshima citizens,
ashes on tongue, sing
what all of us sing.

Veterans Hospital, Moving the Dead

When white-uniformed nurses jolted
the black sailor onto a slab
for scalpels to answer: "Why?"
his limp prick swung,
a questing compass-needle without a way
to know that neither snow-
clothed pole was home.

At the sound of a broom's enmity with earth, South
enlisted her inferior,
the Native American janitor, who'd not,
since the war, helped to rid the world
of such heavy waste.

North's ice-peak nurse-cap loosed,
later, a night-
river a lover could drown in and live in forever,
a morgue-cart whirring for someone,
while hands, that had moved the dead, urgently searched
a face, for a beauty, a possibility
that year, years ago, maybe there.

Veterans Hospital: Terminal Ward

i

A new widow's nails reflecting devotional candles,
a graying nurse disparaging the bereaved's coiffeur,
blizzard bandages what a hospital can not,
while, on the floor buffed
to skating-pond sheen, frost-
uniformed *"fräuleins"* dodge butts,
a gray machine-gunner shooting incendiary bullets
at all he feels
he will not be
worthy—or strong
enough or cruel enough, again—to win.

ii

Survivor of war
and genetic-massacre, a Cherokee sees
Grandmother Spider—her woven basket, pressed
to glowing breast, bearing ungenerous Gods'
fire to us—
while chapel candles' glitters nail
ancestors to air
of a widow's prayers.

Bullet-Holes . . . Drops of Rain . . .

Round bullseye Earth—

I'm five again,
The target my own head,

My father a Redskin cowboy playing at massacring his own—
Most-Indian—son's eventual hordes of descendants,
Meaning to miss me, maybe,
Or only too drunk to shoot straight.

Stalking a dark trail in my mind,
Old enough to shoot back, I find,
The lullaby-singer he had been
And had—whatever he'd wanted to kill in me
Killed in himself—again become.

Sometimes some words strike
My children, despite how I strain
To steady my aim,
A dot a bullet on page, meant
To finish the killer in everyone,
Beginning with me.

My Brother's Aerial Photo of the Farm
where We Were Born

for my brother Rex

Although I've shivered elsewhere,
in higher, thinner and colder air
while strangers' flocks
protected my flesh from fangs
of ice, only in dreams have I flown over home—

where, now, I fly, become
my younger brother, his nuclear-bomber obedient as
a guard-dog to my hand, his eyes
staring through seeming nothing, to find
a former self tending the land,
which frost-faced ancestors conquered from other ancestors,
my brother, as young
as I was when the descendants of lambs
shorn by invading men centuries dead
protected my murderous hands
against the polar wind.

That relentless breath destined to kill
everyone not able to pull
some sort of south around flesh,
this poem is offering,
to all alive or to live, snow
become benign rain,
old dust from volcanoes responding Life,
repeated as Growth
and Change, to endure and keep earth the same,
spring after spring, the tongue
a faithful farmer, tending essential planting—
grandparents and Mom and Dad
and sister and brother, and enemies,
the hardest to cultivate

as friends—where to be
what one must one must
dream on until words become birds,
returning and hatching another clutch of suns,
their singing the singing of everything
offering seed.

Grandfather Wise Wolf at War

Someone in birch-bark canoe
invading my blood, intending to kill me
again, again,
I grope for
millions of shellfish tons
which ocean compressed to war-ax-blade,
in voice I thought mine.

The world, after nuclear-winter, a snowball thrown
at my snow-man head, "Grandchild," is all
I can wield against destruction, love
burgeoning—between commas invisible as the ghosts of sprouts—
into blossoms, of courtship,
of wedding-graduation-victory-and-other-celebrations, and of time
for friends' and families' final eloquence,
echoing on and on and on and, still,
the space will not be filled,
these letters footprints of animals, people or angels
or rain drying in numbers carved into stone.

II

A Man Hunt among the Dead

A robin redbreast in a cage
Puts all heaven in a rage . . .
    from "Auguries of Innocence," by William Blake

for my dad, imprisoned, then pardoned,
for my uncle, Sheriff Dyle Salisbury,
and for a person or persons unknown, who might confess everything

Visiting Poets' Words on Arizona Poetry Center Wall

Decades below

"YEVGENY YEVTUSHENKO," scribbled as high
as huge felt-tip pen could reach
before blurring against ceiling,

my creation—in collaboration with Ingrid Wendt—

eight years beyond conception, further, each day,
beyond parental revisions—

crayoned a rainbow, near
her mother's signature, and her father's fami-
liar Cherokee trick-
ster, Rabbit—a stranger to sky-
strumming claws and earth-
scoring teeth of cacti—only vocabulary, ulti-
mate scream, but—
    boisterous and girlsterous, yip-
    chasing-tail-of-yip,
    anticipation in full cry—
unexplainably able to bamboozle—
    if only in words—
Tohono O'odhams' clever Coyote.

So far
so good! So far
so good! So
long!
Fooled you!
Fooled you,
again.

An Indian Kid's Vision of Snow

for my son Jeff

As sure God made little green apples, the kid is up
to something, but why
he has got the shovel last borrowed to bury his pup,
whose maddening yapping your car made
damned sure didn't grow
louder, you ain't about to give the know-
it-all next-generation
the satisfaction of asking. Then—
like milk-teeth sown
to start a garden of ice-shine dimes,
beneath blizzard-drift pillow—
two rows of snow-blocks grin, and, when
your sweeping of the walk
just happens to move you into view
again a few more times,
it's more or less an igloo risen,
as smooth as that movie's Russian church-dome in
Alaska, from hours the kid spent fashioning it—
with hands doubtless damned near froze—to keep himself
snug like a bug in a polar-bear-rug—
all that work—that could've scraped your driveway bare
as a baboon butt in Africa, for instance—wasted, and damned
if he hasn't got the notion he's one
of his Native American ancestors who fled Asian glaciers,
although he's hardly a decade along a trail
blazed in his genes.

Sun after sun, from milk-tooth-grin,
to colonizers' church, to polar home, snow blocks grow
into multiple-syllable poem's
multiple-molecule trickle, soon to be drowned
in oratory, louder than the ceaselessly gargling sea's,

the frost-faced Northern Hemisphere's population
pontificating conviction that,
beyond its equatorial foundation,
South's half sphere's only a blue pond's
reflection of what is certain
to turn as white
as any racist could wish, mate or kill for—
in nuclear-winter-night—or when the sun
plays out. Somebody Big,
but as full of hell as any kid, will throw
that snowball, and it'll
knock off your hat, as sure as you're born—as sure as
the fucking world.

The Sioux, Their Glory

"Wickiup" is the word, and, about it, the plains
grow buffalo grass
tall as a bull,
rain brighter for each
shoot it has slaked.

"House" has the smug look of brother
jostling another, and "Factory"
could be a father so gone on a toot
he aims his smoking gun straight up—
as too many churches do
bayonet points—not caring who
might be asleep overhead.

"Wickiup," then, breath become a skin-
memorial between the gravestone rows
of teeth, a home walled by air one
of a herd of planets could spare, for all
of us to share.

"Wickiup" again. Sing
of the Sioux, their glory a hide
doomed to become, mid-stride,
another creature's home,
the Sioux moving, as buffalo moved,
spring after spring,
from blade to blade.

After the Treaty

Their smoke thick
as a wolf's gray winter fur
over that from our own box-splinter fires,
under cannon thrust up
like braves' courting boasts,
soldiers stagger out,
and our women go in with them.

I walked all yesterday
to the nearest trees, where elk,
had fought for mates and torn
earth, as invaders had—digging for gold—
our ancestors' graves
and mine.

Canyon de Chelly

Where Americans, in
the name of civilization, and
Conquistadors, in
the name of the Virgin,
massacred Navajo braves in
the womb, Anasazi walls, echoing centuries-
ago-forgotten Athabascan invasion, repeat
and repeat, as if to learn by heart—
for future warning or welcome—
Japanese-shod footbeats of
an Irish-English-Cherokee survivor of nuclear war,
a brother, in prayer, in blood and in hours lived
learning the generations of brick upon brick set
about Kiva, kitchens and beds,
involuntary countryman
of those invading, this time, Vietnam and of
"J. W. Conway . . . Santa Fe . . . 1873,"
boast carved into wall surviving as a confession,
which could have been mine more times than one,
that being is not belonging,
the home he desecrated
one victor's grave stone.

"Among the Savages . . ."

for Father Christian Priber, S.J., and for George Guest,
Gist, or Guess's son, Sikwaya

Atop a frosted Georgia hill as white
as the dome of Sacre Coeur,
a cruciform corn-stalk resurrects
England's Divine Majesty's enemy,
the French priest, Priber, who saved, from flames,
an English prison, then lost,
in it, his "Churakee Dictionary" —
five years of devoted work
"among the savages" — and his life.

A century later, the wife
of Cherokee-German Sikwaya burned
his juice-marked-bark syllabary,
her reason and name
unknown, although she has,
I say, idiomatically,
in English, "gone down
in history," no longer joined
with our language's second lexicographer but
with the first's captors.

My Cherokee dawn-prayers rise —
as Germanic words, which colonized not-so-great-then
Britain — breath white,
like smoke from juice-marked bark or prison, when
the Anglican Church and Rome fought
like dogs over bones,
now dancing, in Earth,
around Sun, thanks
for the gift of corn.

A Poet Knight's Report from the New World

You are tortured. Let's say,
specifically, arrow-tip kernels of maize,
these savages hold sacred,
are hammered into soles then put
to heat, to swell
and burst forth,
like devil's get,
full-grown
at instant of conception.

You,
to be
worthy—not
of liberty but of pain's
surcease
in what awaits
us all—must utter no cry.

"Impossible?"

Chanting their battle deeds
and those of their ancestral clans, they've marched
before these eyes as clear,
I'll swear, as those of any man in Christendom—
feet parodying fishes and loaves—to meet what beat
of heathen drum and spurt after spurt from heart
were promising.

Cutting out tongue,
castration, gutting, drawing, quartering and burning
discouraging opposition
to you, Divinely-Chosen Queen,
at home—here, are misunderstood,
as warrior martyrdom.

What measures, then?

More horse, more cannon, more Englishmen!

Much game, fields, richer, even, than ours
once were, surrounding well-built towns—
and many women quite light-skinned—
God's Truth, Your Majesty,
in but one generation, civilization can begin.

For Sir Walter Raleigh

Rain after rain, off ocean, besieging stone
castles and names above graves
in England, which tribes

from Germany colonized,

a man from land
a sovereign's signature decreed to be
Sir Walter Raleigh's sees
one horizon mast small as a white quill pen,
and ink-worlds, solid as ice, melt
into fathoms of syllables again.

Raleigh, your cloak over mud
and loyalty and bravery nothing to rivals' envy,
your panting and snoring shared
in royal bed led to
your family's bribery's sparing you
torture, your lover-queen's successor
granting beheading, instead, his realm,
like "Vanishing Americans'" chiefdoms, gone,
except in imagination, one
of its triumphs your
freeing the quill
of another slaughtered creature to fly.

A Descendant of "Savage" Nature Worshiper Cherokees Raids Christian Venice

Columbus' countrymen's cathedral filled
with so much gold,
my Indian ancestors understand
why they were tortured to tell where more might be.

"Sex organs cut," in guidebook,
mutilated man and his bereaved's
unborn children's children's children hurl,
onto mirroring canal, a monster structure named
for a saint rocks battered into martyrdom
in Egypt, The Cradle of Western Civilization—
gilded stones so enormous to turn
them into innocent ballast for earth
voyaging around golden sun—and to turn
the Christian religion again into the love, fear
and awe it was born from
would take more life than all
my "primitive" progenitors'
descendants have.

Just below the Snow: Visit to Palace, Bavaria

It's the kitchen that's more
than history—pans shining like captured crowns,
the sense that the whole nation planted
to fill those pans
for one man,

whose portrait has the look
of a youthful Union officer in
the hardly "Civil"—or in
an Indian War—sure he'll impress his girl—
that appetite—and sure he'll survive
heroics, alive—

the king made to drink
a lake, until his ruinous reign
bubbled its last command
as a—denied—request.

A swamp in my lungs—
and tottering from fever—
the sergeant forced me to carry forty pounds
of equipment two miles,
to store it, and march two more
to a doctor, who said,
to someone I could not see, "My God!
I'm surprised he's not dead!"
and I cried at his fatherly tone,
having thought I was o.k.
and just doing what was expected of me,
or anyone, till then.

The second time,
ambulance men and a cop,
finding an Indian Peacenik gasping for breath,
among neighboring Chicanos and Blacks,
took up where the sergeant left off.

Inconsequential. The kingdom continues—
in the snobbishness of tour-guides
and in tourists' can't-believe-their-luck eyes—and needs
a mongrel immortalizer like
a rose needs the lifted leg
of a stray dog.

But one thing I will say—
tour-fee paid, postcard bought,
and all o.k. as far as the native scouts
in my German vocabulary can find out—one thing,
if the shit hits the fan,
as my army buddies used to say,
it's not in this showcase palace I'll lose my scalp,
if I must, but far
above the topmost gilt cross.

A blanket from the royal stable, thicker than those
on the sovereign's bed; the kindling-hatchet; a hunting bow and
that knife beside the butchering-block—I'll go
to just below the snow, and try
to last until new rulers need men
for planting and hoeing again.

A Cherokee Naval History

The Byzantine Navy   TV tells him   planted tree-
dynasties under The Aegean
centuries before his sloop-shape shoes bestrode
the stump-top poop-deck his dad's big saw
had decreed would be a Cherokee history
of green-rigged masts
and yet-to-be-sung Norse heroines, with tresses bright
as dandelions, swimming the lawn.

By sinking into thought, no deeper than
the neighboring volcano's
highest thrown stone
dropped into bed of lake—
which aeons of thaws would eventually create
and other aeons liberate
into clouds shading dried desert muck—
the world's premiere Cherokee sailor has risen again
become one who hurls harpoon-strung imaginings
through days which bend like the curves
of waves, deflecting his resolute aim.

Native progenitors canoeing through
baptismal blood other ancestors' cannon decreed
to be Christian, a bomber's crucifix shape—carved,
into gravemarker air over Nagasaki—
centers a history page black
as space around Saturn's glowing
growth-ringed, fireplace-chunk,

the Byzantine navy sinking deeper than
sun's ultimate taproot's
yearning past Pluto, in
a Cherokee non-sailor–non-historian's brain.

Sacajawea, Bird-Woman, Shows Mrs. America a Native American Diorama

"This one is you—"
tail up beneath
bull-buffalo-shaggy sky, nose
an attachment vacuuming dust-
y trail west, to
yours-for-the-stumbling-over-gold—"you,"
who'd thought you were
each year, a bigger and bigger car's
gem-finish, reflecting:
your house-in-a-row elegant as Great Britain's starch-
shirted parliament or U.
S. nuclear-bombers, whose heavens-lashing plumes
make Sitting Bull's, at his zenith, look
like smoky air, white
around a turkey-butt singed for
Thankstaking—your belly stuffed,
your mind an empty till—
each end-of-day-ray a spear, to the heart
of cocktail-olives, to you.

Against Envy

after *The Sacred Formulas of the Yunwiya*

Moon hatching dark
wings,
owl where the tongue
of a friend had been,
and you, in others' ears, a scurrying mouse, repeat:

Tongue gone into beak,
brain gone into ravenous belly, words gone
into guano, are gone
into tree scarred by sharp feet, gone
into seed, gone
into boards for the homes of the children
of children's children's children, under the sun,
hatching tomorrow's tomorrow's tomorrow.
Ha, ya, yu,
it is so.

Scrub Jays at Feeder

As proud as Custer's,
considering log-barracks castles
compared to teepees,
white skins saints' nimbuses
compared to brown,
sky-uniformed foragers' "Man-
ifest Destiny" is sabering English sparrows,
a Persian, Maltese, Siamese, Burmese or Balinese
the next history.

"Katooah," We Say,

imagining how it was,
the lighter women taken, and the darker,
more fertile, land.

"Kuh too uh," we
mispronounce, most likely,
"the secret society dedicated to tribal purity—"

But Yunwiya now call each other "Cherokee,"
the Choctaw insult name "Cave Men,"
altered by White contempt, the verbal victor.

"Katooah," I repeat
for pleasure of sound—
"Yunwiya," my death,
"Cherokee," rebirth—

and hear "The U.S.," on
a Russian or Asian or Arab's
contemptuous tongue.

Sometimes Likely

If you look white
like I do
and work in the South
like I do
and want to go on making a living for
your woman and children
like I do
there are some
of your people you are
sometimes
likely to forget.

A Historic Denial

A penny saved from the street, Lincoln condemns:
Conquistadors' taking
my Cherokee people's copper
for gold, the U.S. taking back
its given word and, then,
the Native American Siberia, Oklahoma,
for oil, and taking Chile's democracy
for metal, not gold, which Cherokees used for jewelry—
now needed to make, in addition to bombers' circuitry
and jackets for bullets, this coin
as humble as a slave,
its proud public monument not scarred
by "redskin-revenge"
but by municipal macadam,
its Great Emancipator denying—his face
tire-tread-tarred—his race.

III

*Vanishing Americans Battle
to Regain a Vanishing World*

When the lamp is shatter'd
The light in the dust lies dead—
When the cloud is scatter'd
The rainbow's glory is shed . . .
    from "When The Lamp Is Shatter'd," by Percy Bysshe Shelley

And, for all this, nature is never spent;
There lives the dearest freshness deep down things;
And though the last light off the black West went
Oh, morning, at the brown brink eastward springs—
    from "God's Grandeur," by Gerard Manley Hopkins

A *Rainbow of Stone*

Sweat of ascent,
toward Thunder's home,
evaporating in lashes,

a crystalline arc,
erupted aeons ago, glows
like a rainbow,

arc part of a peak,
that's part of a range,
that's part of a world,
that's part of Creation, I climbed
to see more of
more clearly:

factories smoking guns,
a runway a thermometer,
its silver, rising, a bomber,
about to burst into air,
beyond fever, and,

from
horizon to horizon,

my Cherokee people's buffalo, deer,
plantations, even our holy town,
Echota, generations gone.

To crime, monoxide, disease,
and other city uncertainties,

boots pressed to path, blisters to soles, sweat
evaporating off brow,

I must descend,

but,
their stones begotten from fire,
even the arrogant sky-
scrapers will bend,
and,

balled into foetal curl,

the whole earth will be toe-to-toe
rainbows, my own
and Thunder's and your home
again.

Hearing the Famous Talk

of who knew who at Harvard —

    silence of snow
    descending on months
    of snow printed by frost-bitten feet
    stalking an animal's trail
    from the belly of its mother to
    my family's bellies,
    shriveled by hunger —

I study hard,
the wrong
things,
always, all
of my life,
the class I'll fail
aeons of miles down a different aisle.

Around the Sun, the Alaskan Oil Spill

Space-capsule-globules of oil,
their astronauts ghost lizard-birds' coevals,
re-entering the atmosphere
in the nostrils of terns,

I understood my blood,
its cargo vegetable and animal
its red sea-salt surges' mineral,
an ocean of air between poems'
furthest surges and home — understood
a tern may return,
aeons from its last breath, its wings
witch-wings, smothering some other creature —

or I, aeons from words:

which say each tern is sacred,
its flesh to become new life,
to go on sustaining lives;

which say that oil —
formed from the dead — is sacred,
not to be wasted or used
to gratify greed;

which say, with all the breath a mind can hold,
then yield, each moment of life is sacred,
and Timelessness and Death.

Oil Spills, 1966, 1989

In England, which Roman invaders left
my family name, meaning "Town
for Salt" (to keep heat from spoiling meat), I was fed

by a grant (conceived to prevent poets'
extinction) the year a tanker,
ironically from the Romans' old home, split
against Land's End,
like a napalm-bomb, and spilled-oil killed
flora and fauna enough
to have filled many Legions' bellies,

a year of The Vietnam War,
an Arab defeat in Israel,
and Nigerian massacre of Biafrans.

On land Spirits intended to keep
my Indian people from extinction, I killed —
twelve to eighteen, before the army — meat
enough for my family.

No electric-lines for refrigerator,
no radio and no tv,
salt and our family's stories
preserved what we needed to live
and to die, in time, at peace
with the creatures whose lives we'd made ours.

OIL SPILLS, MORE CARS, OIL WARS
and SUICIDAL MURDERERS' BULLET HOLES
IN CHILDREN'S CHILDREN'S CHILDREN'S
OZONE PROTECTION, our literature
today, tomorrow's a page

as white as a nuclear-winter night,
to be written on,
I pray, by a Hand warmer than mine.

Ocean Enough: Exxon's Alaskan Oil Spill

Drowned by black blood of creatures extinct
except in our engines and brains, a bird—
whose genes might have sung
in his species forever—reminds me I may be "Tsi-skwa,"
Yunwiya for "Bird Clan"
"Tsaragi, Tsalagi, Cherokee" names
"Yunwiya" 's become
in the mingling of genes and tongues.

No mingling of oil and water.
A cup of the former will seal
waves' surface and calm, I'm told,
in English, ocean enough to save a ship,
but "spilled tons" translated as
"THE PRICE OF PROGRESS," won't save the future's
ancestors who've disappeared unconceived.

Having hunted one species of prairie-chicken extinct,
my and my people's "lesser of evils," that kept
us from starving during The Great
American Depression,
a hunger stronger than anger moves me to say,
reverently, "Tsi-skwa," pronouncing it "See-squaw,"
my family's way, thinking of mating, and birds
who may not ever be born
sing fossil-fuel pterodactyl
from engine, from ocean, from corpse-poisoned shore
into air, "Tsi-skwa" a ghost-
fledgling again,
to fly and, in time, in time,
to again die, in a last descendant's ear.

Oil Spill Spreading

Confessing, first, I'm a killer,
a carnivore, and that I shot
at creatures of my own shape
attacking my home in a night as black as the sun
drowning in oil spilled in Alaska,
I speak of elephants,
which words in the world's
least likely to be extinct languages protect—
starting the month of my birth,
next year, the slaughter to be greater, like oil
put under pressure, till then,
months piled on centuries of wasting mountains of meat
on a starving continent.

One can understand a neighbor's missiles' frightening another
to self-preservation;
however, our fellow mammal, the largest alive on land's
means of protection lures murderers,
as aeons-under-stone animals and plants,
transformed to "Black Gold," lured whites
to steal the American "Siberia" imprisoning Indians,
where oil company guns
won Dad's union's election.

Three sons soldiered for capitalism, but one
of them—Earth hurtling toward extinction—tries
to power survival with sounds
derived from voices of centuries of tons
of flesh—ink black
as fossil-blood on a white
Alaskan shore
in danger of being, forever,
the night of nuclear-winter.

The Ultimate Mountain

"to see the world in a grain of sand,
eternity in an hour"
William Blake

We think it's night sky
in the skin of a grape

We think it's revival
bigger than tent

We think beyond thought
miraculously huge and strange
each grape the dome
of the ultimate mountain
the seething volcano-cathedral-dome seeks
to become.

Through Nothing

Start with the green   sun
Plunges through aeons of nothing
To reach   or with
An ancestor's mating cry's
Echoing the future's
History   which you will be   air warmed
By phallic lunge   in time   a poem
Imagination trying   to overcome
Tyrannical fact   old civilizations
Too civilized to survive
Fleeing to dream   sun nuclear then
As now   plunging to warm green
That rays not become armies
Unborn   fleeing through aeons of nothing on and on.

The Violet that Killed a Mountain Sheep

The beauty, solitary on promontory's, to die,
not from one sunrise more
than flesh can bear,
nor from money hunters have spent for sport,
but from rarity,

its fatal enemy
the Flett Violet,
which grazing endangers.

A Cherokee survivor,

my belly maybe the last
nest of a prairie chicken species one
too many like me
ravenned extinct,

feet sensing holds in stones,

I hunt, merely to see,
a brother-killer, its petals the blue
through which a helicopter bears,
dangling from an umbilical attached to natal-sac,
generations of deadly, beautiful browse's
beautiful peril away.

For a Prairie Chicken, Now Extinct

Its shape somewhat like a bullet,
my trigger-finger, which squeezed
so many living shapes
into dinner plates—
now's

a worm,
curled around this stem,
my scribbles roots,
petals invisible
wings

of a prairie chicken,
that almost flightless, easily killed bird,
the last mouthful of its meat maybe mine,

who flew in a bomber like the one
which put a small Japanese city into history.

Until and After

Miraculously here—after centuries
of efforts to destroy
our kind of creature—see:

a brain-sized bird—unable,
almost, to fly—red meat
tough for the milk-teeth, with which I chewed
and chewed, not to starve
too long and grow ill
and, like my brother, be still,
without being told. See—

its only defense, brown-leaf-camouflage-feathers,
stark against black plowed-earth—the last
Iowa prairie-chicken, the Ioway Indians
intended should live forever—the slow,
easily-killed game salvation for hunters in blizzard,
even as porcupines are, even today,
in the American north, and, in Iran,
the ancient religion Mohammed destroyed
prohibited killing them. See—

gray growing white—a Cherokee survivor
of nuclear-war, who has prayed, with his body
and brain, for a bird—
its spirit—and would pray
for our kind, that we may live
as well as we are able, until,
and after, the extinction of the sun.

For Simon Ortiz

Engine eager, creators' ancestors sensing kin,
migrated generations ago—
and, yet,
my small Asian car could only get
half way up the road
a movie crew had left,
to twist like a rattlesnake's sloughed skin, beneath Sky
City, where Simon Ortiz remains
always at home,

while his words circle the world,
suns warming North Pole
and South at the same time,

and lies,
frozen so hard
they seemed Truth,
melt,
ascending, becoming
Sky City's neighbors in sky
then falling, slaked growth blessing earth's
centuries of people, Simon's
and ours, again.

Continuing Sikwaya's Search

for Gayle Tremblay and for Sikwaya, who fashioned
the first written access to a native North American
language, Cherokee, and who died, old and revered,
still searching for our people lost in Mexico after
fleeing massacre by European Americans

Twenty and wary of revealing her Indian identity,
in those days of racist oppression, Gayle Tremblay,
seemed summed by the suggestion of her name,
as rendered orally, but,
now, when my search for our people, lost
in the massacre inflicted by Time, seems
hopeless, again
and again, she's there—
uptrail ahead of me, alone,
as she always was, and as all
must, ultimately, be,
but leading an army of our tribes,
women and men, out of the years,
centuries and, even the aeons, when
the sum of the oral tradition was wind's
persuasion of minerals and rain.

For Ed Edmo, Shoshone-Bannock

Ed Edmo's so from where he's from if you buried him, untaken
scalp to calluses thick as Wapiti moccasin soles, he'd grow and
grow and grow a forest around him, protection from civilization's
soul-killing wordsontv and gene-shriveling bombs, a forest, walnut,
apple, ponderosa pine.

Jim Barnes, Choctaw

Leading, tethered to his tongue, a pony Spaniards left the Choctaw,
on its back, in a deerskin pack, everything trucks could not hold,

Jim Barnes is trading the world: clothing, food, weapons, for hunting
and for defending, his take: glass beads, small as Christmas tree
baubles, so fragile they shatter just from the jolts of passing time, so
worthless even the European pony shakes its head, so ordinary even
pony piss in a hoofprint is equally shiny, so traditionally the trick
invaders played on the gullible Indians, even existing governments,
contemptuously ignorant of poetry, are surprised to discover the New
World, the Old, the Great Globe and the Universe, being borne
away, being borne onward, being, being, being borne home, inside
the grinning trader's artfully packed hide.

In Memory of Bill Stafford, Good Indian, Who Fought to Save Crow's Feet's Band and Other Survivors

Alone, and armed
with a peace pipe, he
was scouting the enemies in
his genes, and in
the centuries of English history's
colonization of each new American generation's minds in
universities, when,
after winning all the Indian Wars
he could, by losing the parades,
he found himself
leading more brothers and sisters than he
or anyone on this battleground,
our society, had thought
alive. Completely, wholly, surrounded, he fought,
as the young pacifist he'd been had fought, with
and for everyone, by giving Up
and Upside-Down
and, above all, Always
Beyond-bounds, a second, a third
and, yes, an infinite chance, until,
summoned by Sun—
for council, accolade, well-deserved rest
or who knows what—
to our mind-freezing sorrow our words try
to insulate out, he went.

For One of Us, Lost while Climbing

"now, if you're lost enough to find yourself"
Robert Frost

Boot a comet nudging planets from orbit, eyes try
to find sign other than his own, in
disruption of stream-bed stones'
aeons-in-forming constellations.

Green compass-blades
bent, beneath weight,
to seek earth's center or
the comfort of roots'
intricate confusions of directions, grass—
a survivor of more than metaphor—
risen again, from posture of prayer, toward
altar-step clouds, shows how
a climber must go, to go
on being a climber, all of us to follow, as far
as any of us knows, and further, one is
not sure but can, tested to the utmost, hope.

Lava—so solid soles, in comparison, seem,
falling and rising feathers—erupting, became,
again, Earth's primal mineral dream of birth from Sun,
whose going down and dawning, scientists say, will,
eventually, both be gray—
and midday—then dark,
burned out, whatever nuclear soldiers do—
yet moving, in accustomed circles—like one
whose riches are gone,
no longer able to give, only to beg,
borrow or steal off relatives—
learning humility from moons
and other orphans, who, turning to black,

blank album-page, discovered the ultimate progenitor,
too old to smile or frown,
neither benign nor other, but there,
the climber thinks out loud, breath steaming air, thinned by its
ascent from earth,
even as he has climbed and thinned, lost,
but only for a time, in a universe—which matter is said
never to leave or enter—the furthest shining galaxy as real
as Golden-Mantle Ground Squirrels
flashing the splendor of their Creator,
scampering from wing-shadow into the den
of the climber's deepest vision, his own—
and perhaps only—salvation, his pulse
the ticks of the clock on his wrist, black beaks
circling to strike.

Vieques, after Hurricane Hugo

Stormed bare as Sahara dune,
the reef next door's barnacled again,
by TV antennae,
balconies, awnings and air-conditioners, and beds,
deposited, in layers, like silt, beside the street,
their pillows as wrinkled as brain-
coral, still hollowed by shapes of years of heads,
will all be gone
before refugees are driven here,
from turbulences news-named L.A.,
Chicago, New York.

My wife's and my only neighbors, so far,
are trilling and strutting and ruffling, to mate,
and cats, black clouds on horizon, dream
the dreams storms dream,
while realtors' cars, as sleek as sharks, swim sun,
their feeding-frenzy again begun.

A *Liberation and a Farewell to Arms*

Pen-point a foetal fingernail or
a possibly remotely ancestral insect-mandible
learning magnetic North Pole compass-needle's far
from certain circling
in possibly-to-end-up-baffling whorls
of pulp-paper's source, beneath bark, I am
freeing my eyes
of bomber-scrawled sky,
freeing my life
of tree's progression from towering to toppling,
freeing my flesh from roots'
temporarily necessary intestinal-tangle.

Though a tick in Eternity's
armored-brigade's gears' grinding, wrenched,
by the centuries of romantic poetry's prick-
and-cunt-evasions, out of,
and in the nick of, time, I am
the pause an orator makes before
decreeing war—thrust
of a bayonet
back into scabbard, rust—
minerally meek,
like all save the cerebral chemicals—
eventually to be victorious.

A fingernail, having survived
the need to be trimmed,
popping first pimple of youth
and learning again,
from aeons of latitudes and longitudes,
the nothing a suitor hears
as "yes," I trust my next breath,
the stretching of skin over lungs, over teeth, inside ear,

an airplane arriving in time,
a hand learning more of what Creation has planned than
the brain of anyone who is other than a lover can.

To Sing of the Sun,

Take "North"
      take "West"
Take "South"
      take "Dawn"
On tongue;
    and,
Singing one,
      sing all
Of the dead
      creatures you've ever seen,
Become,
    in song:
      first robin, breast last
Coal's glow,
      bloody beak match
Struck
      against glass invisible as air,
Crimsoning
    to flame,
      glass blazing this summer morning
You've sung of,
    sun
On your whole,
    alive,
      body
A part of your future
      winging across vast blue,
That blue—
    despite all armies can do—
To be there, to be there
      in your eyes, and you—
Become new,
    become earth

Become worm,
  become robin —
To be there,
  to be there,
Forever,
  for all you know.

Out of Sleep under Stars

Waked by my scent riding night's cold wind
        the horses   that love to eat
            from hands

the grass they could crop
        between their hoofs

neigh me from dreams
        my childhood's hunger become

bear startled out of hibernation   starved
        for shivering colts   nestled as deep inside
            my warm sleeping bag as words and years
                and a barbed wire fence will let them get.

Skyful of Teeth

Four-hundred-pound-force hurtling fear
at the cub of another species, boy
now grown, hears roar become sea
devouring shore,
black fur black breakers
reflecting black sky, and,
teeth meteors, dawn,
exploding from gun, is blood
of a starving hunter's first feast, on
a bedtime-story-telling tongue.

Yunwiya Initiation Hunt: For Quarry Greater than Bear

I am hunting, hunger my gut's growl
another hunter will—by being eaten or by eating—still.

As a cub learns,
from parental enamel's channeling
of lives of other creatures, I learn
from my father's
channeling of breath into words
to guide
steel's lethal channeling of air,
that lead should find meat.

Nuclear-winter's endless hibernation
channeling life into extinction,
parents and children are growling again,
and nothing will still all
of those stalking and stalked,
my tongue one of the ones
by which they may be fed.

A Father's Bear Dream

Between my teeth,
I am
carrying a child,
over new-fallen snow,
through freezing air,
   an alert bear
   with only a few more gray
   bushes of breath
   to burgeon and disappear
   to be
   safe
   for a time, among
   deep dens of the Old Ones, and
my fear
   of awakening,
   of running out of ink,
   of being driven away,
   with nothing to say,
   borne,
I must go beyond the end of the trail
my parents made,
my feet in their tracks,
their child between my teeth,
a few breaths, maybe, more until we're there.

Fall Hunt for Winter Meat

Skull shattered, shot
splintering into echoing,
venison runs for a few seconds more
of its own dawn-shadow-lengths,
gust of the final hurtle stirring fertile volcano dust
to erupt into wind and whirl on and on, to,
finally, heavy with rain, descend
and become, season after season, browse
for generation after generation, where, before,
for aeons and aeons, only stones'
shadows fell.

Rare Plant Viewed after TV Nature Special
and Commercial

Smog-grayed leaves rough hides—
bees birds feeding off rhinoceri—
and curved thorns horns
panderer poachers pulverize
to make men breed
oftener—fossils burn
to their second extinction,
hastening Earth's,
while tv mating-simulations
sell cars. It seems natural to see some
of an endangered and
endangering species
as blood-colored petals curved thorns impale.

Frost Baby Harp Seal Pelt,

The first tulip bud's now blood
Gasped into furrier-floor-flood dawn—the dawn

That pulsed in my family's poultry, then
In slender blizzard-drift shape I clubbed
And pried out of trap-teeth baited
With guts of victim-chicken.

This weasel, I killed for wasting our breakfasts
Before they were laid,
Our dinners not yet hatched—
And whose beautiful skin I will sell—
Draped on my arm,
Thirteen and Indian, I'm
Escorting an expensive woman.

Incredibly wealthy—
And older by more than time
Since my war-club descended—
With armies to command, how can I feel
I am only a survivor of massacre
After massacre—as all are—and were—
Even before Hiroshima—small bag,
Beginning thin hair between skinny legs,
My people's pitiful hope?

Wife and our daughter, 13, in dreams, I woke—
Sun tulip, in window's faint frost then blood-drench—
My nightmare: weasels,
Which kill for the thrill of killing
And leave an entire winter's need
To the appetite of earth.

It is terrible, another animal as insane
As Man. Terrible, the seal babies red as tulips on snow
Slopes curving like graceful shoulders white
As the days and days between Arctic—or before
Nuclear—nights.

A *Harvest of Rainbows*

Starvation in winter my childhood and death
of my brother, this summer, Calcutta streets strewn
with bodies, pitifully thin, I'm living
each moment I'm dying, I'm thankful
I'm working, I'm feeding my children, my future: clouds'
glistening seeds, to grow
into rainbows, a harvest which could be my last.

Above Dinosaur National Monument, Utah

Climbing too high,
eyes on far peaks, which point
a possible way deeper into sky,
boot-edges flay
a thin skin of clay
slipping for hundreds of meters of fear,

till hands become claws,
forearms and shins
bellies of lizards, and down
on a designated trail
past centuries of petroglyphs, I hear the stone
flutist's silent admonishment
to go where feet were meant to go
on faring and dancing while air
mouth shapes into song or prayer ascends
beyond the tallest stone.

IV

Death Songs

So shalt thou feed on Death, that feeds on men,
And Death once dead, there's no more dying then.
   from "Poor Soul, the Centre," by William Shakespeare

One short sleep past, we wake eternally,
And Death shall be no more; Death thou shalt die.
   from "Death Be Not Proud," by John Donne

Six Prayers

Thunderer   God of the turbulent sky   may
my turbulent mind shape
for my people
rain clouds
beans
pumpkins
and yams.

East Spirit
Dawn Spirit   may
birds awaken in
the forest of teeth
whose river   your color   must say
frozen mountains'
prayer that you
will loosen them.

Spirit of the North
whose star is our
white mark
like the blaze we chop in black bark
where the trail home
divides
even in
our homes
we need
you to guide.

Spirit of the Sunset West
may gray clouds
hiding friends from me
glow
like yours
that we grope

toward each other through
a vivid rose.

Spirit of the South
direction of
warm wind
warm rain
and the winter sun
like a pale painting of a morning glory
help me   Spirit   that in my mind humble things
a man may give to his child may grow
the blue of berry
orange of squash
crimson of radish
yellow of corn
when the green of even the tallest pine
is wolf tooth white.

Spirit of the Earth
keeper of Mother Father
Sister Brother
loved ones all
once praying
as I pray
or in some other way
Spirit   the black dirt
is like the black cover of
a book whose words
are black ink I can
not read
but I place my brown hand
on snow
and pray that more than snow
may melt.

The Only Medicine Sure

for Chicabob, my father's mother's mother, and for John
and Mary Ax, who ministered to our people

My dad, did he say anything, did he say,
a prayer so old the words
were ones he
had not ever heard,
his mother's mother's breath
blown from his tongue,
with smoke from tobacco,
the Medicine Hummingbird had suffered—throat
to glow like a lighted pipeful, forever—to win
for us, from selfish or testing Gods—and did I—
my ear-drum almost burst,
from centuries of pain
aeons of evil spirits inflicted on
untold numbers of listeners in human genes—did I hear
Grandmother's parents' parents' prayers,
to be shaped, warmed and sung in my own generation?—

the only medicine sure
whatever we give when we try
to give more
than the Gods alone
seem able to give.

Burning the Old Garden Fence

A ghost of woods Greatgranddad's ax massacred—
his gun one of the ones which felled
my Indian forebears—this post
survived winds stampeded,
from North Pole tethers,
down longitudes' quaking lanes
and survived brute tons of pork-
generations' attempts to invade
the garden, and, although

unable to survive, forever,
persistent termite teeth
of the same rains
which turn the earth
to grain, to milk,
to flesh and bone, in brain,

this teetering survivor may still survive
my saw's methodical mineral-intent,
as fire-place-smoke, as black
as youth's untamable Vanishing American hair's
free-verse tangle.

Other ancestors' gunpowder cloud's
white page combed,
with Shakespearian Sonnet exactitude,

Greatgranddad's trigger-finger aims pen
at my imperialistic, militaristic time's
perpetuation of his,
his wife-wooing, child-comforting hands
sprouting from wrists,
as I hunt for one memory more

of love and try to fence ghosts
in—the only way I know
to try to pray.

To My Father's Mother

Your pine above

> a smoke-stack-forest,
> whose poisoned river curves
> like a silver dollar sign—

your pine above

> a grave among Cherokee graves
> your children were
> too Christian to bury you in,
> as you'd pleaded—

for you,
and for all of our people,

a tree frog sings from

> this house whose walls may be
> grandchildren of your pine.

For Mary Turner Salisbury

The only surviving panes,
    were World-War-One-
    and-Great-American-Depression-
    news, she'd slicked with animal fat
    to protect her home
    from cold and rain, and sun
    made spider-webs glow Rapunzel gold
    around a wheel, spinning a yarn
    of another century's rich plantation, doomed
    to be sustained, not
    by treaty, "as long as the rivers shall flow," but
    by family story, as long as family remember.

Arms, which had cradled and raised
    twelve sons and two orphaned grandsons to manhood,
    by then, as thin as the shovel-handle,
    sixteen, I harvested her hard clay sweet-potato patch,
    guilt-free that day,
    I must honestly say,
    as I've seldom been—

between sweat's rainbows
    in lashes: cruciform warplanes, my
    Manifest Destiny:
    two years of cruel confusion
    in one of them.

A Violet in My Fist for My Mother's Mother

From rhythms as regular as rows
raised on your farm so that meat,
itself to be eaten, could eat,

known
as loving words my mother's girlhood sobs
became,
Grandmother, know

one grandson

as petals, fed,
by parents centuries in earth —

these petals I offer a stone
chronicler of your suffering
cancer and having to leave your child
before she — unlike my own — was grown.

Mine gone, into her
home's blossoming, a hull
is her mother's and my
reminder of two others, in time,
to neighbor your own.

A teacher as ignorant as Socrates knew
himself by knowing himself to be, I live
on lives an aeons-gone glacier —
in groping, miles short of equator — left
to take root beneath rain ice,
in its resurrection, became,

my hope: that you may see—
through six feet of dirt
and the vision of a grandson,
at times pitilessly blinded by erudition—your
greatgranddaughter's picture, drawn
on the way to the graveyard and scribbled
"To speshul parents from a speshul girl,"
a gift as fragile as petals fragrance I leave,
and, groping, words short of all I think
I intended, still receive.

To My Mother's Father

Grandfather, your own
mathematically clear, in stone, my years
are berry brambles tangled over hide-and-seek,
rotting-back-into-roots wood-shed,

which held summer enough
to keep four children alive
till the first violets opened
windows and doors, and your wife,
till cancer, a rat in the potato bin, ate her
share of the warmth.

My other granddad abandoned an Indian wife,
twelve children and honor, but,
your son-in-law's stories and songs struggled,
through end-of-the-day exhaustion, to be mine
and now struggle, to become
a paean for your daughters, Aunt Jenny and Mom,
both of whom soothed
six children's coughing or scary dreams for hours,
after days of hard work.

Grandfather, under fly-specks and toothpaste flecks
as gray as petals of old funeral bouquets,
the father of three's eyes see,
your white mustache and hair
in this motel mirror,
your grandson, his family visiting done,
on his way home.

What Grows

This may be my mother's birthday
I know it was May
and there had been eighty,
that spring I sent the last
roses she'd ever breathe
on this earth,
as far as I know,
which is as far
as my own next breath.

I believe, from what grows
as naturally as roses, I love her, and,
surrounding darkness stirring, flesh
her flesh and Dad's formed
shrivels toward becoming
petals or thistles, bright stars
still rooting in layers of a grave
I have gratefully breathed since
my first birthday
slap.

For Years and Years

Both times in your car

First   as you drove slowly behind me until
    on legs no longer than pencils it seemed
first grade had not taught me to move right   I reached
the lane of my home   and you might have meant nothing or
to scare any memory of Grandfather's love
from our farm you had not inherited

The next time was war   90 deaths in my head 90 or more
I forget   it was war   and they might have been candles
or wood on a grate
and   on my way home   I might have been anyone
in uniform and needing a ride
and when you learned my name then said "I'm your aunt"
I remembered the other car

and I see my mother
teetering at the edge of the ditch ahead of us
little legs like charred stems in black stockings
books cradled like kindling
and lunch-bucket-bail a monstrous wedding-band
gouging through mitten though only weighted by
stale smells

"Run over her" I scream   this is not a car
and you are dead   as is she
and I know by now she forgave you
grew fond of your son   and that love and hate
are sisters or brothers and war
is too grown to be either   and rage
    as I scream   machine gun in hand   "Run over her God
Damn you if you dare"   is rage at death

and   even as I write this   at five in the morning
    my daughter   who's seven   screams out of sleep
for the first time in months   and my anguish was hers
    my poem her nightmare   or only pure chance
and the way the world is
and the way the world is   I
whisper   pencil not
moving right
yet   "Don't run over her.   Please.   Please.   Go slow.
Go slow.   Don't run over her
or me, for years and years."

Dad's Old Plowing Buddy, Met

Bowed to still sheets, Dad's
old friend, a name, only, till then,
says if he's next he's ready,
so old, he's ready.

We children, grown
out of innocence
into a trinity
of pagan believers, stare
at two hundred pounds of what had been
air squeezed into our ears,
now rising, full size, to again raise out of earth
ahead of plow, stones heavy as those
flesh which created and fed our flesh
must molder to ounces under.

May I—

not ready, heart pumpkin out of rhythm
with the season, mind maize
Spain murdered Cherokees
to steal, transplanted hands
of bananas my clustered words
trying to ripen faster than frost
can kill shooting-star petals—

may I have
enough to give
to deserve to be raised,
from time to time, on someone's tongue
as air more nurturing, more enduring or
anyway lighter than stone.

A Harvesting

Brown and curling around a finger of air,
this fern frond's my papoose fist,
still only urge in earth's
aeons of growth when seed
yearned to ascend, from roots,
to song, Dad's thumb strumming
iced vines above his grave,
frost melting from
season on season of English, Irish and Cherokee tunes,
fist finding trigger-finger, the hunt
for food, for generations,
now harvesting with tongue,
then pen, the feasting, dancing, courting again begun.

*

Cherokee Ghost Story: My Father's

Their whisky, women, dancing and clouds
    of their greetings fading in cold wind,
the stranger, pale astride—
    a mount as white
    as reflected moon
    they'd turned thirsty horses toward—rode
full gallop through flesh, pierced
by arrows of enemies decades dead,
    answering gunshots echoing in
    a meteor-crater the young
    men ride,
decades of words,
    from the tongue
    of the son of one of them.

As Day Was

I'd know him

by boulders, plow'd grate against
like milk-teeth grinding meat
and finding shotgun-pellets he'd aimed,
as our ancestors aimed stones,
to harvest dinner from air.

Words wings to keep
quail flying and children growing and
hunting and feeding children again,

I'd know him,

from hands
that moved boulders a glacier had plowed
from Arctic strata and borne south,
with generations of miles of migrant vegetation I knew
as the loam of my family's farm.

I'd know him

from banjo strings strummed
and lullabies sung
against fears of a night
as black as day
was bright.

Noise of Going-to-Work Traffic, London:
Accidental Deaths

This morning's absent-minded greeting from
my old English-poet host's like one from my
Kentucky-ballad-singer Dad—

five fingers, five senses, searching five banjo-strings
as crimson as veins, in dawn,

exploring five sunrise rivers for

the tunes of Old England, or—
from Kentucky's deep mines and Cherokee farms
eroding off hills—a new one,

his 64th year,
his last,
nodding "Good morning" that morning a child,
he'd thought grown, killed
the young ballad-singer, weapon a plea
for a lullaby he'd live more
bachelor years
and towns, as adventuring minstrel, before
he'd be ready to know.

Home To

for my brother Ray

One skunk caught
    in scent on wind

another skunk   caught
    killing chickens
    again's a black
    and white bagful
    of rifle bullets
    in years-ago snow.

My older brother I hunted
    those days with's a
    demanding teacher still
    his he-man body slumped
    over sissy heart   the fall
    of his gray head
    jerking me 2000 miles
home to
    stark white and black.

The Color Of

for my brother Leland

Green gopher's gone underground,
as if a plump shoot had been plucked
down by the roots,
although it's only escaped to its den.

I'm ten.

There's a pheasant the colors of dawn
it flew through, sky-rag in my daddy's hand
to wipe from their plates
his family's hunger for a time.

And one will be eleven,

his brother under toes
which crawl like field-mice as brown as autumn blades
not fast enough,

while clouds drop leaves
the color of
the feathers of
his pet duck
the hunger of
something plucked under
river skin shuddering in wind.

This Is My Death Dream

I'm three. I'm balancing
the family barn
on my thumb, and
I'm thickening inside,

all of my cells
even my brain
thickening.

This is the doctor
who's done all medicine can
and fever will either break or I'll die.

This is my dad,
an ice storm of tears on his windshield.

Though late night roads
are drifted almost closed,
and though there's no money for meat
he makes the dangerous journey to town, for
a treat, I'm
too weak to eat.

Let him leave ice cream by my grave till spring
wilts it,

and let my gratitude bloom by his,

though, drunk, he'll shoot
around my feet, old wood's new white
splinters the thorns of a crown
in the picture above the hallway mirror.

Barn teetering huge on
a crescent moon black
beneath nail, these are the animals, terrified
I'll drop them
to smash amid kindling.
How can they know
that fever from
the heavens will burn
their home before I'm grown, and
the only way they'll be saved
is for me to survive
lightning and war
and remember them.

This is the thickening.
It's maybe as if all the days of my life
are crowding like loved ones into a poem
or citizens fleeing
a city about to be bombed
by B-24s I'll fly in for 26 months 300 hours
see 200 die and 27 years later still feel
myself in one
plane named "Flying Barn"
teetering on invisible thumb.

By Then

Streetlights a scattering of freckles,
One bright window a scar,
It seems familiar, the hill
Across the valley from
This home I have begun
To buy, with a Veteran's loan.

Maybe my own
Illuminated window's a scar
To the distant neighbor awake,
As I write, worrying for my sons,
Endangered by new war,
Dawn soon to stain—
A firing-squad wound—white-bandaged sky.

Only one real cartridge was loaded,
Secretly, by a compassionate officer, to save
His soldiers from guilt,
I remember and remember the kindness, as well
As the cruelty, of many,
Some staring a fourth of a century, now,
As the wood roof of their final bunker gives in
Under relentless machine-gun-spatter of rain.

My only visible
Scar, the pale path of a knife, recalls,
An anachronistic American Indian war
Against the conqueror.
Hidden, that interrupted chalk-scrawl, my spine,
Is flight-recorder evidence "human-error" caused
A bomber to crash.

Generations ago, we Cherokees
Were buried the way
I have had to train myself to sleep,
In foetal curl, pain
Bone carved on a nerve
Commanding that I not ever again
Bury the back of my head in a pillow—
Eyes up at stars freckling sky—until
All pain ceases—the hill,
Asleep under its freckles and scar, the face—
I hope—of an old
Old friend, by then.

A Name on a Tombstone

"word of mouth . . . the oldest and best idea that man
has of himself . . . which, because it was never
written down, was always but one generation
from extinction . . ."
    from *House Made of Dawn*, by N. Scott Momaday

Refrigerator's hum
a distant bomber's motors, I
remember trying to sleep away debauchery,
parachute pillowing dark
head propped against vibrating bomb-bay door
till after Nagasaki
released me to marry.

My son's rocking his crib's
the rhythm of Dad's banjo strummed,
a last time, and lullabies sung, to sound again,
in descendants' dreams,
when my pillowed head's
all white, my name
on stone, erosion, sung
to generations of strumming rain.

Long and Longer

It doesn't even get away,
The Big Fish, but—

Year after year of snow's
Melting and plunging toward ocean—

It swims deep
And deeper, as I cast, and casts
Into depths, among shadows, a shadow I
See always and
Always downstream from
My long and longer—as the day
Grows shorter—own.

One Past

I will put my earth-brown hand
    with its shell-crater-crested-highest-hill knuckle
    infantry won
    and with knife-scar-valley palm's white-ice-river—

I will put my five-winged, flightless,
    one-past-the-last-of-the-dodo-birds
    hand
    down,

    to become another doomed-for-extinction metaphor,
where snow-page-scurrying, black-beak-pen-tip sipped a—
    hopefully—late fall's final trickle.

Gentle in Green

Breathe pine, destined for dwelling,
See eyes, taste lips, touch thighs.

For coffin, breathe oak, veins bones
Of ancestors shadowed in leaves because the One
The fiercest among us can
Not ever stare down's
As gentle in green
As the nothing
Which can be said.

Thanks You

You go with some sadness, that's true,
but the stones of the stream go, also,
seeking, your feet say, stones' stairway home
beneath ocean as blue as
the glittering shadow of God—

knowing, by this time,
no foot sinks through air
its shaft of warmth
alone,

for always there are carseats
encouraging lovers,
airlines uniting the unlikeliest would-be-angels,
wheelbarrows bearing mortar to
an office-building's awkward adolescence,
and even the sun,
under its terrible burden of vacuum,
thanks you for being someone
for it to lean upon
going down.

Closer

My first mountain here,
in the air of Father's voice,
in his name
on stone, sends down
centuries of tons of snow,
to splinter, to campfire kindling,
a structure, where
some ancestors prayed
some others off earth, sky,
year after year
closer, over my nose.

If Anyone Does

My wife—who knows me if anyone does—
I'm telling her more than I know, my hope
that it may be so,
this time, this rhyme
as reassuring as the next
heart beat, my tongue
trying to make all o.k.—my death
a sequence in centuries of occurrences—a perspective:
that I was almost killed
younger than our daughter is now.

Her mother grieving for when I'll be gone, I try
to reassure,
syllables tears between whiskers—salt on my tongue,
preserver of meat—
a blessing that feet can feel carpet, arms
a shape of warmth
as familiar as hope
my grave only the door
to strangers, so far.

Death Song, My Own

When I die, time will be still
the same for all
who loved me and
for all. My climb,
to the Great Spirit in the sky,
will seem no further hurtling of the stars,
no rocket shot beyond the moon,
but only toss of pebble into pool,
those I would kiss, joke with,
cuddle—or try, again, to kill—
beautifully shadowed ripples filled with sun,
a final, faint erosion touching shore.

Acknowledgments

Some of the poems in this collection have previously appeared in the following anthologies: *Returning the Gift* (University of Arizona Press), *Songs from This World on Turtle's Back* (Greenfield Review Press), *Durable Breath* (Salmon Run Press), *A Season of Dead Water* (Breitenbush Books), *Crosscurrents* (an anthology of poems by poets who teach), *Literary Olympians* (an anthology of American poems published in an Olympic year), and *The Clouds Threw This Light* (Institute of Indian Arts Press); and in the following magazines: *The Amicus Journal, Andrews Review, Anthropology and Humanism, Calapooya Collage, Chadokoin Review, The Chariton Review, Centering, The Colorado Quarterly, Confrontation, December, Fireweed, Greenfield Review, Hawaii Review, Negative Capability, New Renaissance, Northwest Review, Oregon East, Poet and Critic, St. Andrews Review,* and *Silverfish Review.*

About the Author

The son of a Cherokee-English father and an Irish mother, a quarter-blood Native American, as the government nowadays reckons ethnicity, Ralph Salisbury has written two books of stories and five books of poems that relate his family's stories and his experience of the often violent contemporary world in which he has survived. *Rainbows of Stone* reflects his devotion to the Cherokee religion, its fidelity to forebears, and its harmony with the forces of Nature. As the book suggests, his spirit life is involved with a commitment formed after his being struck by lightning at age fifteen. Ecology, social justice, awareness of Cherokee history, and opposition to war are major aspects of his work.